Easy-to-Preach
Sermon Outlines

Easy-to-Preach
Sermon Outlines

Russell E. Spray

BAKER BOOK HOUSE
Grand Rapids, Michigan 49516

ISBN: 0-8010-8313-3

Third printing, April 1994

Printed in the United States of America

Scripture references are taken from the King James Version of the Holy Bible.

Contents

Foreword

Easy-to-Preach Sermon Outlines is designed to give help, time wise, to busy ministers in their sermon preparation. These outlines are also both easy to listen to and easy to remember.

It is my prayer that those who deliver these messages and those who hear them will be blessed, and God will be glorified.

1

Be a Confident Christian

"I can do all things through Christ which strengtheneth me" (Phil. 4:13).

You can be a confident Christian. Here's how:

I. The Positiveness

"I can" (Phil. 4:13).
A. "I can" is a positive affirmation. Reject negatives. Accept positives.
B. When it comes to doing God's work, many Christians have said, "I can't" until they are robbed of confidence.
C. To become confident Christians, we must abandon the "I can'ts" and begin thinking and saying, "I can" accomplish for God—as Paul did.

II. The Performance

"do all things" (Phil. 4:13).
A. The apostle didn't say, "I can do some things" or "I can do a few things." He said, "I can do all things."
B. Some Christians are lax when it comes to doing anything to advance God's kingdom here on earth. Some are lazy. Some, fearful. Some, unconcerned.
C. We gain confidence by entering doors that God

opens. He is always present to assist, enable, and bless as we "do all things."

III. The Person

"through Christ" (Phil. 4:13).
A. Paul's secret for success was: "through Christ." His accomplishments were performed through the power and might of God, not through his own strength.
B. We also must recognize that our accomplishments come "through Christ." We must act totally in the will and power of God lest we fail.
C. Be a confident Christian. Step out in faith. You will be amazed at what you can do "through Christ."

IV. The Power

"which strengtheneth me" (Phil. 4:13).
A. The apostle Paul's sufficiency was not found in himself. He recognized Christ as the source of his strength.
B. Of ourselves, we are nothing. But if we act in faith, assured that Christ is working through us, we need not fail, for he cannot fail.
C. God's Word admonishes, "being fruitful in every good work . . . strengthened with all might, according to his glorious power . . ." (Col. 1:10–11). You can be a confident Christian.

2

Christians Should
R-E-A-C-H Forward

". . . forgetting those things which are behind, and reaching forth unto those things which are before" (Phil. 3:13).

I. Reach Forward with R-eliance

"And the Lord shall help them . . . because they trust in him" (Ps. 37:40).

A. Some Christians rely too much on other people, possessions, pleasure, and popularity. They lack spiritual victory. They're doomed for disappointment.

B. We must reach forward with reliance on God, the only one who never fails. He promised, "I will uphold thee with the right hand of my righteousness" (Isa. 41:10).

II. Reach Forward with E-njoyment

"Happy is he . . . whose hope is in the Lord his God" (Ps. 146:5).

A. Many Christians wear long faces and possess negative attitudes. They displease God, discourage others, and dispirit themselves.

B. To be the blessing we should be, we must reach

forward with joy. "Rejoice in the Lord alway: and again I say, Rejoice" (Phil. 4:4).

III. Reach Forward with A-nticipation

"And this is the victory that overcometh the world, even our faith" (1 John 5:4).

A. Anticipate means "to look forward to; expect"— Webster. Christians should reach forward with faith.

B. Some want to believe—after they see things happen. Jesus said, "What things soever ye desire . . . believe that ye receive them, and ye shall have them" (Mark 11:24).

IV. Reach Forward with C-onstancy

"But he that shall endure unto the end, the same shall be saved" (Matt. 24:13).

A. Some Christians do well when everything goes their way, but they throw up their hands in defeat if it doesn't.

B. Reach forward with constancy. Keep on keeping on. Never give up. Keep your eyes on Jesus. He endured the cross for us. (Heb. 12:2).

V. Reach Forward Toward H-eaven

"I press toward the mark for the prize" (Phil. 3:14).

A. All Christians expect to reach heaven. Our eternal goal should be "the prize of the high calling of God in Jesus Christ," like Paul's was.

B. Jesus said, "In my Father's house are many mansions. . . . I go to prepare a place for you. . . . I will come again, and receive you" (John 14:2–3).

3

Christians Can Be Conquerors

"Nay, in all these things we are more than conquerors through him that loved us" (Rom. 8:37).

I. By Living in Christ

"if any man be in Christ, he is a new creature" (2 Cor. 5:17).

A. Christians are in Christ. They are new creatures in him. "Old things are passed away." "All things are become new."

B. Many Christians lack victory because they do not continue to live in Christ. They neglect prayer, Bible study, and church attendance.

C. To become conquerors, we must keep ourselves in a spirit of prayer daily. According to the Scripture, we are to "pray without ceasing" (1 Thess. 5:17). And we must claim God's promises as our own.

II. By Leaning on Christ

"Trust in the Lord . . . lean not unto thine own understanding" (Prov. 3:5).

A. Some Christians do not trust the Lord completely. They lean on their own strength or that of others.

B. To be victorious, we must trust the Lord implicitly and lean on him completely. He must be our daily hope and help.

C. The psalmist said, "And the Lord shall help them, and deliver them . . . and save them, because they trust in him" (Ps. 37:40).

III. By Laboring with Christ

"We then, as workers together with him" (2 Cor. 6:1).

A. Many Christians lack victory because they are remiss when it comes to doing God's work.
B. Some are too busy with personal pursuits. They lack the time and concern to do God's work.
C. Be a conqueror. Take time for the Lord. Be ready to lend a helping hand, speak a kind word, give assistance to the homeless, and witness to the lost about Christ and his power to save (Matt. 6:33).

IV. By Loving Through Christ

"And walk in love, as Christ also hath loved us, and hath given himself for us" (Eph. 5:2).

A. Some Christians are self-centered and self-seeking. They fail to walk in love as they should.
B. To be pleasing to God, Christians must deny self and increase in love and compassion for others.
C. We can be conquerors by loving others through Christ. God's Word admonishes, "Let us not love in word, neither in tongue; but in deed and in truth" (1 John 3:18).

4

Describing the Christian L-I-F-E

"I am come that they might have life, and that they might have it more abundantly" (John 10:10).

I. L-oving Life

"Thou shalt love the Lord thy God with all thy heart . . . soul . . . strength . . . mind; and thy neighbour as thyself" (Luke 10:27).

A. Many Christians fail to love God and others as they should. They are self-centered and too busy seeking personal gain.

B. We must deny ourselves, showing lovingkindness to the sick, lonely, and elderly. We should give of our means to assist the needy and less fortunate.

C. The scripture admonishes, "Be kindly affectioned one to another with brotherly love" (Rom. 12:10).

II. I-nspiring Life

"I will extol thee, O Lord; for thou hast lifted me up" (Ps. 30:1).

A. God lifts his people when they pray and claim his promises.

B. He inspires them with the hope of eternal life. "In hope of eternal life, which God, that cannot lie, promised before the world began" (Titus 1:2).

C. Christians should be an inspiration to others. Their

life and testimony should be a blessing to other Christians and inspire sinners to seek the Lord.

III. F-aithful Life

"Mine eyes shall be upon the faithful of the land, that they may dwell with me" (Ps. 101:6).

A. Faithful means: "Keeping faith; maintaining allegiance to someone or something; loyal"—Webster.

B. Many fail when it comes to being faithful. They neglect everyone and everything for personal pursuits.

C. We must be faithful to God, family, and others, giving of our time, talent, and treasure. A crown of righteousness is promised to the faithful (Rev. 2:10).

IV. E-ternal Life

"And this is the record, that God hath given to us eternal life, and this life is in his Son" (1 John 5:11).

A. The "more abundant life" includes eternal life. We deserved to die. "For the wages of sin is death" (Rom. 6:23).

B. God gave his only begotten Son to die on the cross for our sins. "The gift of God is eternal life through Jesus Christ our Lord" (Rom. 6:23).

C. We must repent and believe on the Lord Jesus Christ, and God will give us eternal life (John 3:15–16).

5

Draw Near to God

*"Draw nigh to God, and he will draw nigh to you"
(James 4:8).*

I. Sense God's Presence

*"But it is good for me to draw near to God: I have put
my trust in the Lord God" (Ps. 73:28).*
- A. Many Christians fail to sense God's presence
  because they do not commune with him in prayer.
- B. Some Christians neglect their prayer life because
  they are too occupied with secular interests, or
  because they underestimate the necessity of fellowshiping with God.
- C. Prayer is a must for Christians. Through prayer we
  communicate with God, enjoy his fellowship, and
  sense his presence (Ps. 37:4–5).

II. Search God's Promises

*"Search the scriptures; for in them . . . ye have eternal
life" (John 5:39).*
- A. The Bible, God's Word, is too often neglected by
  many Christians. Through it he draws near to his
  children and we draw near to him.
- B. Search his Word. Find those special passages
  which fit your needs. Study them. Memorize them.
  Claim them.

16

C. Paul said they "were written for our learning, that we . . . might have hope" (Rom. 15:4).

III. Seek God's Peace

"Seek peace, and pursue it" (Ps. 34:14).

A. Many Christians get caught up in the stress and conflicts of today's world. They try to cope in their strength and fail.

B. We draw near to God by learning to depend on him. Take everything to him in prayer with thanksgiving. Leave all your burdens with him, too (Phil. 4:6).

C. The promise is ours: "And the peace of God . . . shall keep your hearts and minds through Christ Jesus" (Phil. 4:7).

IV. Sing God's Praise

"Sing forth the honour of his name: make his praise glorious" (Ps. 66:2).

A. Most of us are negligent when it comes to praising God. We simply forget or neglect.

B. There is no better way to praise the Lord than to sing his praises. We draw near to him through song. We would do well to follow King David's example.

C. One psalmist admonished, "Sing unto the Lord, bless his name; shew forth his salvation from day to day" (Ps. 96:2).

6

God Speaks to His People

"The Spirit himself beareth witness with our spirit, that we are the children of God" (Rom. 8:16).

I. God Speaks Through Prayer

"He shall call upon me, and I will answer him: I will be with him in trouble; I will deliver him" (Ps. 91:15).

A. In Old Testament times God sometimes spoke directly to his people. In this Holy Ghost dispensation, God speaks to us through the Holy Spirit.

B. God speaks to us when we pray. While fellowshiping with him in prayer, we sense his presence and peace.

C. Christians are bidden to "pray without ceasing" (1 Thess. 5:17; 1 John 1:3).

II. God Speaks Through His Promises

"Whereby are given unto us exceeding great and precious promises: that by these ye might be partakers of the divine nature" (2 Peter 1:4).

A. Skeptics have ridiculed the Bible for centuries, but it has never been outmoded or destroyed (Matt. 24:35). It offers hope to humankind (Rom. 15:4).

B. The Bible, the true Word of God, is his message to his people. Through his Word we receive the promise of salvation, sustenance, and stability.

18

C. The Bible contains promises for our every need. We must read them, reread them, remember them, and rely on them. God speaks to us through his Word.

III. God Speaks Through His Preachers

"For it is not ye that speak, but the Spirit of your Father which speaketh in you" (Matt. 10:20).

A. God's Word was written by holy men. "All scripture is given by inspiration of God . . . . That the man of God may be . . . throughly furnished" (2 Tim. 3:16–17).

B. God spoke through his preachers of the past—Luther, Wesley, Moody, Sunday, Stowe, and others.

C. God speaks through totally committed messengers today, those who practice and preach the Word of God.

IV. God Speaks Through His Providence

"And we know that in all things God works for the good of those who love him" (Rom. 8:28, NIV).

A. Providence means: "The care or benevolent guidance of God"— Webster.

B. God speaks to his burdened people, comforts the sorrowful, and gives power to the faint (Isa. 40:29).

C. Great strides have been made in science and medicine, but these do not compare with the miracles and blessings God sends to his people.

7

God's G-R-A-C-E Is Great

"And with great power gave the apostles witness of the resurrection of the Lord Jesus: and great grace was upon them all" (Acts 4:33).

Grace is "the unmerited love and favor of God toward man"—Webster.

I. His G-oodness Is Great

"O give thanks unto the Lord, for he is good: for his mercy endureth for ever" (Ps. 107:1).

A. Through his great grace, God's goodness is revealed to humanity. He loved us while we were still in sin.

B. The psalmist said, "For thou, Lord, art good, and ready to forgive; and plenteous in mercy unto all them that call upon thee" (Ps. 86:5).

II. His R-edemption Is Great

"By his own blood . . . having obtained eternal redemption for us" (Heb. 9:12).

A. Because of God's great grace, our redemption was obtained through the blood of Jesus Christ.

B. Salvation awaits those who come to God in genuine repentance and faith (Eph. 2:8).

III. His A-ffection Is Great

"For God so loved the world, that he gave his only begotten Son" (John 3:16).
A. God loved us so much he gave his only Son to die on the cross for our redemption, paying the price for us.
B. Paul said, "God, who is rich in mercy, for his great love wherewith he loved us . . . (by grace are ye saved)" (Eph. 2:4–5).

IV. His C-are Is Great

"Casting all your care upon him; for he careth for you" (1 Peter 5:7).
A. Today's world offers little personal attention and care. Most people are too busy to help anyone else.
B. God is never too busy to care for his own. The psalmist said, "Cast thy burden upon the Lord, and he shall sustain thee" (Ps. 55:22).

V. His E-ndurance Is Great

"But the mercy of the Lord is from everlasting to everlasting upon them that fear him" (Ps. 103:17).
A. God's great grace doesn't last just for a day, a week, a month, or a year. His grace is eternal.
B. Paul said, "That in the ages to come he might shew the exceeding riches of his grace in his kindness toward us through Christ Jesus" (Eph. 2:7).

8

God's Grace Is Sufficient

"And he said unto me, My grace is sufficient for thee: for my strength is made perfect in weakness" (2 Cor. 12:9).

I. Sufficient in Trials

"That the trial of your faith . . . might be found unto praise and honour and glory" 1 Peter 1:7).

A. Many Christians make it fine until trials come. Then they throw up their hands in despair.

B. God's grace is sufficient in trials. He allows them to come to us to strengthen our faith, but each trial is first screened by God's love (1 Peter 4:12–13).

II. Sufficient in Troubles

"The righteous cry, and the Lord heareth, and delivereth them out of all their troubles" (Ps. 34:17).

A. Life today is filled with trouble. Family, church, and world problems abound everywhere.

B. God is still in control. His grace is sufficient no matter what happens. He has promised to be our "strength in time of trouble" (Ps. 37:39).

III. Sufficient in Testings

"Behold, Satan hath desired to have you, that he may sift you as wheat" (Luke 22:31).

A. Satan desires to possess and control Christians today. Like Peter, he waits to "sift them as wheat."
B. God's grace is sufficient in times of testing. We must trust God implicitly, keeping the faith. Jesus told Peter, "But I have prayed for thee, that thy faith fail not" (Luke 22:32).

IV. Sufficient in Temptations

"The Lord knoweth how to deliver the godly out of temptations" (2 Peter 2:9).
A. Temptation is one of Satan's choice tools. He used it against Adam and Eve in the garden. He still uses it.
B. Praying and trusting Christians need not be defeated. "God is faithful, who will not suffer you to be tempted above that ye are able; but will . . . make a way to escape" (1 Cor. 10:13).

V. Sufficient in Tribulations

"Rejoicing in hope; patient in tribulation; continuing instant in prayer" (Rom. 12:12).
A. Webster defines tribulation as "great misery or distress, as from oppression; deep sorrow."
B. Tribulations are common in today's society, but God's grace is sufficient to keep his trusting children. He wants us to commit ourselves totally to him (Rom. 12:1).

9

Go in God's Strength

"I will go in the strength of the Lord God" (Ps. 71:16).

I. Go with God's Presence

"Lo, I am with you alway, even unto the end of the world" (Matt. 28:20).

A. Sometimes Christians falter because they lack the assurance of God's presence. They feel alone and lonely.

B. God's people are never alone. He is with them and has promised never to leave nor forsake them (Heb. 13:5).

C. The scripture admonishes, "Draw nigh to God, and he will draw nigh to you" (James 4:8). Draw near to God in prayer and go with his presence.

II. Go with God's Promises

"For all the promises of God in him are yea, and in him Amen" (2 Cor. 1:20).

A. Many Christians do not succeed because they neglect the promises of God, failing to appropriate them to their needs.

B. God speaks and directs us through his Word. We should be diligent about using the promises of God.

C. We must go with God's promises. They inspire,

enlighten, and empower us on our journey through life (Ps. 119:105).

III. Go with God's Purpose

"According to the eternal purpose which he purposed in Christ Jesus our Lord" (Eph. 3:11).

A. Some people go through life with little or no purpose. They merely exist from day to day.
B. To be successful, life must have a goal. There must be a drive and reason for being, doing, and going.
C. Our purpose should be to glorify God. We must do his work with diligence. Be ready to assist the less fortunate and witness to the lost. Go with God's purpose (1 Cor. 10:31).

IV. Go Through God's Power

"Strengthened with all might, according to his glorious power" (Col. 1:11).

A. Some Christians attempt to go in their own strength and fail. Finite strength is insufficient for today's demands.
B. We must have God's infinite power if we are to successfully accomplish the tasks we should perform.
C. Go with God's presence, promises, and purpose, and through his power. "I can do all things through Christ which strengtheneth me" (Phil. 4:13).

10

How to Be a Blessing

"For in him we live, and move, and have our being"
(Acts 17:28).

I. Live and Move *in* Christ

"Therefore, if any man be in Christ, he is a new creature" (2 Cor. 5:17).
A. Christians "live and move" in Christ. Forgiven, they are new creatures in Christ.
B. Christ also lives and moves in totally committed Christians. His Holy Spirit cleanses and fills them with God's love (John 17:23).
C. The Holy Spirit gives direction to those who "live and move" in Christ. He empowers and enables them to perform their daily tasks and glorify God (Acts 1:8).

II. Live and Move *like* Christ

". . . leaving us an example, that ye should follow his steps" (1 Peter 2:21).
A. Many professing Christians do not "live, and move" like Christ. They continue to live selfishly.
B. To be a blessing we must strive to be more like Christ. Pray. Read God's Word daily. Practice faith, hope, and love while walking in his ways.
C. Christ left his example that we should follow him

in our thinking, seeing, hearing, speaking, doing, and going (1 Cor. 6:20).

III. Live and Move *for* Christ

"Thou therefore endure hardness, as a good soldier of Jesus Christ" (2 Tim. 2:3).

A. A good soldier "lives and moves" for the nation he serves. He is ready to sacrifice his life to protect his country and those he loves.

B. To be soldiers of Jesus Christ we must be ready to endure hardness, sacrificing ease and pleasure, to serve the Lord.

C. To be a blessing we should "live and move" for Christ. He gave his life for us. We must deny ourselves, take up our cross, and follow him (Matt. 16:24).

IV. Live and Move *with* Christ

"Lo, I am with you alway, even unto the end of the world" (Matt. 28:20).

A. Christians "live and move" with Christ in the present. He promised, "I will never leave thee" (Heb. 13:5).

B. Those who are a blessing and "live and move" with Christ today will be privileged to "live and move" with him in the life to come (1 Thess. 4:17).

C. Christ has also promised to return and claim his own (John 14:3).

11

How to Have Peace

*"Peace I leave with you, my peace I give unto you. . . .
Let not your heart be troubled, neither let it be afraid"
(John 14:27).*

I. Think Peaceful Thoughts

*"Thou wilt keep him in perfect peace, whose mind is
stayed on thee" (Isa. 26:3).*
A. Many Christians lack God's peace because they
continue to think stressful and fearful thoughts.
B. We must surrender our tensions and fears to God
and claim his promise: "The peace of God . . . shall
keep your hearts and minds" (Phil. 4:7).

II. See Peaceful Sights

*"Looking unto Jesus the author and finisher of our
faith" (Heb. 12:2).*
A. Millions of people watch the danger and destruction displayed on television and the movie screen.
B. If we are to live in peace, we must look to Jesus.
He promised, "Peace I leave with you" (John
14:27).

III. Hear Peaceful Sounds

"Faith cometh by hearing" (Rom. 10:17).
A. Many lack peace because they constantly listen to

loud, lewd music. Their spiritual reserve is exhausted.
B. To enjoy peace, we must hear wholesome and uplifting sounds. And, we should listen for God's voice. He often speaks in "a still small voice" (1 Kings 19:12).

IV. Speak Peaceful Words

"Talk ye of all his wondrous works" (Ps. 105:2).
A. Many Christians fail to talk about the goodness of the Lord. Instead they criticize and find fault.
B. To have peace we must speak kindly, remembering that "A soft answer turneth away wrath" (Prov. 15:1).

V. Perform Peaceful Deeds

"In every good work to do his will" (Heb. 13:21).
A. There are many needy people in today's world. Some are sick, elderly, and unable to care for themselves.
B. Peace awaits those who lend a helping hand to others. Everyone can comfort someone (Prov. 3:27).

VI. Attend Peaceful Places

"I was glad when they said unto me, Let us go into the house of the Lord" (Ps. 122:1).
A. Many Christians attend places displeasing to God. Their Christian influence is damaged.
B. Christians must be watchful about the places they frequent. They need to go where God is glorified (Prov. 4:18).

12

How God Reveals His Promises

"Whereby are given unto us exceeding great and precious promises: that by these ye might be partakers of the divine nature" (2 Peter 1:4).

I. We Must Read God's Promises

"Order my steps in thy word: and let not any iniquity have dominion over me" (Ps. 119:133).

A. Many Christians fail to avail themselves of God's promises. They forget or simply neglect to read them.
B. God speaks to us through his Word. If he is to order our steps, we must know what he has promised.
C. The psalmist wrote, "O how love I thy law! it is my meditation all the day" (Ps. 119:97).

II. We Must Retain God's Promises

"I will never forget thy precepts: for with them thou hast quickened me" (Ps. 119:93).

A. Some Christians read God's promises but fail to retain them. They fail to receive their full benefits.
B. To retain God's promises, recall them throughout the day, write them down, or refer to them often.
C. The psalmist said, "Seven times a day do I praise thee because of thy righteous judgments" (Ps. 119:164).

III. We Must Rely on God's Promises

"Thou art my hiding place and my shield: I hope in thy word" (Ps. 119:114).

A. Webster says that rely means "to have confidence; trust . . . to look for support or aid; depend."
B. The scripture says, "There hath not failed one word of all his good promise" (1 Kings 8:56). We should recall them, rest on them, and rely on them.
C. The psalmist relied on God's Word. He said, "Thy word is a lamp unto my feet, and a light unto my path" (Ps. 119:105).

IV. We Must Rejoice in God's Promises

"Thy testimonies have I taken as an heritage for ever: for they are the rejoicing of my heart" (Ps. 119:111).

A. The psalmist rejoiced in God's Word. He said, "I will delight myself in thy statutes: I will not forget thy word" (Ps. 119:16).
B. Many Christians read the promises out of a sense of duty, but they fail to rejoice in them.
C. God honors his people with his promises. We are privileged to claim them as our own. God reveals his promises to those who read them, retain them, rely on them, and rejoice in them.

13

How to H-E-A-R from God

*"He shall call upon me, and I will answer him: I will be
with him in trouble; I will deliver him, and honour him"
(Ps. 91:15).*

I. H-eed God's Word

"I will never forget thy precepts" (Ps. 119:93).

A. If we are to hear from God, we must heed his
Word. Study it. Believe it. Receive it into our
hearts.

B. Many Christians neglect God's Word. They lack
divine instruction and direction for their lives.

C. God's Word leads us and guides us. According to
Ps. 119:105, "Thy word is a lamp unto my feet, and
a light unto my path."

II. E-njoy God's Work

*"With good will doing service, as to the Lord, and not
to men" (Eph. 6:7).*

A. Some Christians falter when it comes to doing
God's work. They are too busy making a living and
caring for other personal concerns.

B. God's presence and power for service accompany
those who do God's work joyfully. Eternal rewards
are also promised (1 Cor. 15:58).

C. Paul said, "And I will very gladly spend and be

spent for you" (2 Cor. 12:15). We should work diligently and gladly for God's cause also.

III. A-ccept God's Will

"Nevertheless not as I will, but as thou wilt" (Matt. 26:39).

A. Many people are set in their ways. They insist that things go their own way.
B. If we are to hear from God, if we are to please him, we must accept his will. It is always right and best.
C. Through prayer and reading God's Word, we can find God's will. The psalmist said, "I delight to do thy will, O my God: yea, thy law is within my heart" (Ps. 40:8).

IV. R-eflect God's Ways

"When a man's ways please the Lord, he maketh even his enemies to be at peace with him" (Prov. 16:7).

A. Some Christians seem to reflect Satan's ways more than God's. They are remiss where prayer and Bible study are concerned.
B. God reveals his ways to us through his Word. We exemplify Christ when we reflect God's ways.
C. God's presence and peace accompany those who reflect him. He promised, "Blessed are they that keep my ways" (Prov. 8:32).

14

How to Increase in Love

"And the Lord make you to increase and abound in love one toward another, and toward all men" (1 Thess. 3:12).

I. Think with Love

"Whatsoever things are lovely . . . of good report. . . . think on these things" (Phil. 4:8).
A. Many Christians are lax when it comes to thinking loving thoughts. It's easier to dwell on the bad.
B. To increase in love we must replace negative thoughts with positives, dwelling on the good. (Phil. 2:5).

II. Listen with Love

"The righteous cry, and the Lord heareth, and delivereth them" (Ps. 34:17).
A. Christ listens with love to the sinful, needy, and hurting of this world. He hears their faintest cry.
B. Like Christ, we must listen with love to the sinful, suffering, and sorrowful about us. (Mark. 4:24).

III. Look with Love

"He beheld the city, and wept over it" (Luke 19:41).
A. Christ looked with compassion on the sick, sinful, and less fortunate (Matt. 9:36). He is the same today.

B. To increase in love, we should look on the faults and failures of others with compassion, being ready to forgive (Heb. 12:15).

IV. Speak with Love

"A soft answer turneth away wrath: but grievous words stir up anger" (Prov. 15:1).
A. Too many Christians speak harsh, unkind, and critical words. They are lacking in love for God and others.
B. We increase in love by using words of faith, hope, love, consolation, and understanding (Eph. 4:32).

V. Labor with Love

"Remembering without ceasing your . . . labour of love . . . in our Lord" (1 Thess. 1:3).
A. Christ's work was a labor of love. He comforted the bereaved, healed the sick, gave sight to the blind, and forgave the sinful.
B. Our love increases when we give smiles, say kind words, do good deeds, and witness to the lost (1 Cor. 15:58).

VI. Walk in Love

"And walk in love, as Christ" (Eph. 5:2).
A. Christ walked in love. He went where he could be the greatest blessing and glorify his heavenly Father.
B. Millions of people follow after selfish pleasures and pursuits. We must work for God and others (Isa. 48:17).

15

How to Please God

"Make you perfect in every good work to do his will, working in you that which is wellpleasing in his sight, through Jesus Christ" (Heb. 13:21).

I. Expect the Presence of God

"Draw nigh to God, and he will draw nigh to you" (James 4:8).

A. Some Christians fail to expect God's presence because they neglect to fellowship with God.

B. Few, if any, Christians always feel God's nearness. To expect his presence is to believe for his presence.

C. We please God when we expect and accept his presence by faith. He promised, "I will never leave thee, nor forsake thee" (Heb. 13:5).

II. Explore the Promises of God

"That ye be not slothful, but followers of them who through faith and patience inherit the promises" (Heb. 6:12).

A. God promised to multiply Abraham's descendants but the promise did not come to pass immediately. Abraham waited with faith and patience until it did (Heb. 6:15).

B. We must explore the promises until we find those that suit our personal needs, then, accept them as our own. Like Abraham, we must wait with faith and patience. God's timing is always best.

C. God is pleased when we accept his exceeding great and precious promises. We become partakers of his divine nature (2 Peter 1:4).

III. Experience the Peace of God

"Peace I leave with you, my peace I give unto you. . . . Let not your heart be troubled, neither let it be afraid" (John 14:27).

A. Many Christians lack the peace God offers. They worry and fret about temporal possessions and pursuits.

B. It pleases God for us to have his peace. It is his will for us. Jesus said, "My peace I give unto you." We must accept his peace.

C. God's Word promises perfect peace to those who keep their minds on and trust in the Lord (Isa. 26:3).

IV. Express the Praises of God

"While I live will I praise the Lord" (Ps. 146:2).

A. Most Christians fail to praise the Lord enough. Some neglect; some forget; some are too busy. God is displeased.

B. All heaven praises the Lord. The angels and God's host praise him continually. We need to begin now.

C. The psalmist said, "I will bless the Lord at all times: his praise shall continually be in my mouth" (Ps. 34:1).

16

Jesus Christ the D-O-O-R

"I am the door: by me if any man enter in, he shall be saved, and shall go in and out, and find pasture" (John 10:9).

I. D-irect Door

"I am the door" (John 10:9).

A. Some people think they must go through another person to reach God. They lack a personal relationship with him.

B. We can go directly to God through Jesus Christ. By prayer and through God's Word we have direct access to the Lord.

C. Jesus said, "Come unto me, all ye that labour and are heavy laden, and I will give you rest" (Matt. 11:28).

II. O-pen Door

"By me if any man enter in, he shall be saved" (John 10:9).

A. Some doors are open to a certain clique, race, or creed but are closed to those who do not meet their requirements.

B. Jesus Christ, the door, is open to all who come to him. The great and small, rich and poor, black and white alike are welcome, for with God "there is no respect of persons" (Rom. 2:11).

C. We must come to God in simple, trusting faith. We must forsake our sins and believe on the Lord Jesus Christ, accepting him as Savior and Lord (John 3:16).

III. O-nly Door

"For there is none other name under heaven given among men, whereby we must be saved" (Acts 4:12).

A. Some doors lead to popularity, some to pleasure, and some to possessions. Jesus Christ is the only door that leads to salvation and eternal life.

B. Some try to gain heaven by accomplishing good works, performing good deeds, and giving to the less fortunate. God's Word says, "Not of works, lest any man should boast" (Eph. 2:9).

C. Enter the only door, Jesus Christ. Work as unto him, giving him first place (Matt. 6:33).

IV. R-edemptive Door

"I am come that they might have life, and that they might have it more abundantly" (John 10:10).

A. Humankind sinned and deserved to die, for the wages of sin is death.

B. Jesus Christ gave his life on the cross for us, the just for the unjust. He took our place (John 10:11).

C. Jesus Christ is the door to redemption and eternal life (Rev. 3:20).

17

"My Jesus, I L-O-V-E Thee"

"We love him, because he first loved us" (1 John 4:19).

I. L-ifting Love

"My Jesus, I love Thee; I know Thou art mine. For Thee all the follies of sin I resign. My gracious Redeemer, my Savior art Thou. If ever I loved Thee, my Jesus 'tis now"—first verse of the hymn, "My Jesus, I Love Thee."

A. When Christ was on earth, he lifted the sick, blind, lame, and sinful. He lifts sinners out of the miry clay. He promised to "stablish, strengthen, settle" Christians (1 Peter 5:10).

B. Our love should lift others also. We should be ready to encourage the discouraged, comfort the sick and lonely, and share Christ with the unsaved.

II. O-bedient Love

"I love Thee because Thou hast first loved me, And purchased my pardon on Calvary's tree. I love Thee for wearing the thorns on Thy brow. If ever I loved Thee, my Jesus 'tis now"—second verse of the hymn, "My Jesus, I Love Thee."

A. Christ's love was obedient. "He humbled himself, and became obedient unto death" (Phil. 2:8).

B. We should serve him obediently, loving him with all heart, soul, strength, and mind (Luke 10:27).

III. V-ictorious Love

"I'll love Thee in life, I will love Thee in death, And praise Thee as long as Thou lendest me breath; And say when the death-dew lies cold on my brow, If ever I loved Thee, my Jesus 'tis now"—third verse of the hymn, "My Jesus, I Love Thee."

A. Christ's love is victorious over death, hell, and the grave. "Death is swallowed up in victory. . . . O grave where is thy victory" (1 Cor. 15:54–55).

B. Our love should be victorious over trials, troubles, and testings. We can also be victorious in death. We need not fear death, for Christ is our victory (1 Cor. 15:57).

IV. E-ndless Love

"In mansions of glory and endless delight, I'll ever adore Thee in heaven so bright; I'll sing with the glittering crown on my brow, If ever I loved Thee, my Jesus 'tis now"—fourth verse of the hymn, "My Jesus, I Love Thee."

A. Christ's love knows no end. It is from everlasting to everlasting. "God is love" (1 John 4:8, 16). Heaven will be permeated with God's eternal love.

B. Christians who are filled with Christ's love here below will enjoy heaven where love abounds eternally (John 14:1–3).

18

Pleas for Direction

"Shew me thy ways, O Lord; teach me thy paths. Lead me in thy truth" (Ps. 25:4–5).

I. "Shew Me"

"Shew me thy ways, O Lord" (Ps. 25:4).

A. Today's society offers a variety of options to choose from—the way of self-seeking, the way of sinful pursuits, the way of Satan worship, and God's way.

B. The psalmist prayed that God would show him his ways. God's ways are always right and best. We should choose his ways.

C. God's Word guides us. We also find God's way through prayer, meditation, and by trusting God for direction.

D. The scripture admonishes us, "In all thy ways acknowledge him, and he shall direct thy paths" (Prov. 3:6).

II. "Teach Me"

"Teach me thy paths" (Ps. 25:4).

A. Some Christians lack God's direction because they are set in their own ways. If we are to receive God's guidance, we must be teachable and willing to learn.

B. We learn about God's paths by studying and learning from his Word. Science, psychology, and philosophy cannot take the place of believing, preaching, and living the Bible.

C. Jesus said the Holy Spirit "shall teach you all things, and bring all things to your remembrance, whatsoever I have said unto you" (John 14:26).

III. "Lead Me"

"Lead me in thy truth" (Ps. 25:5).

A. There is a great need for the truth in today's world, which is filled with false religions and doctrines. David prayed for God to lead him in his truth.

B. If we are to be led by the Lord, we must live in his presence. He promised never to leave nor forsake his own (Heb. 13:5).

C. Jesus promised that the Holy Spirit would abide with us forever. He dwells within the totally committed Christian. He shows us his way, teaches us, and leads us (John 14:16–17).

D. The Holy Spirit will lead us into the truth. "When he, the Spirit of truth, is come, he will guide you into all truth" (John 16:13).

19

"Secret Place of the Most High"

"He that dwelleth in the secret place of the most High shall abide under the shadow of the Almighty" (Ps. 91:1).

The "secret place of the most high" is

I. A Place of Devotion (Ps. 91:1–4)

"He shall cover thee with his feathers, and under his wings shalt thou trust" (Ps. 91:4).
- A. Many Christians neglect their devotion to God. They fail to communicate with him and read his Word.
- B. We should continue in a spirit of prayer at all times. Select and use the promises of God that help you.
- C. The text says, "He that dwelleth in the secret place" shall live in God's presence (Ps. 91:1).

II. A Place of Daring (Ps. 91:5–8)

" A thousand shall fall at thy side, and ten thousand at thy right hand" (Ps. 91:7).
- A. Many Christians are afraid to do God's work for fear of criticism or a lack of self-confidence.
- B. We must be brave. Dare to do things to glorify God and be the blessing that he wants you to be.
- C. The psalmist said not to fear the terror, the arrow, the pestilence, or the destruction about us. God shall protect his own (Ps. 91:5–7).

III. A Place of Defense (Ps. 91:9–13)

"For he shall give his angels charge over thee, to keep thee in all thy ways" (Ps. 91:11).

A. Ours is a dangerous world. It is filled with divorce, drug abuse, destruction, terrorism, and murder.
B. Millions, even some Christians, live in fear. Christians should not be afraid, for God is with them. God is omnipotent, and he is our defense.
C. The psalmist wrote, "Because thou hast made the Lord . . . thy habitation; There shall no evil befall thee" (Ps. 91:9–10).

IV. A Place of Deliverance (Ps. 91:14–16)

"Because he hath set his love upon me, therefore will I deliver him" (Ps. 91:14).

A. Many Christians are bound by self-doubt and the opinions of others. They fail to be the blessing they should be and thereby fail to glorify God.
B. Satan is going about as a roaring lion seeking whom he may devour. But "we are more than conquerors through him that loved us" (Rom. 8:37).
C. The psalmist said "He shall call upon me, and I will answer him: I will be with him in trouble; I will deliver him, and honour him" (Ps. 91:15).

20

The Dynamics of Trust

"Trust in the Lord with all thine heart; and lean not unto thine own understanding" (Prov. 3:5).

I. The Who of Trust

"O taste and see that the Lord is good: blessed is the man that trusteth in him" (Ps. 34:8).

A. Some Christians place too much trust in doctors, lawyers, ministers, or friends. Man is infinite and subject to error. Trust in man brings disappointment.

B. We appreciate the help we receive from others, but our ultimate trust must be in God, who is infinite and unfailing.

II. The What of Trust

"nor trust in uncertain riches, but in the living God" (1 Tim. 6:17).

A. Many Christians put too much importance on making money and acquiring possessions. The scripture warns about the "love of money" (1 Tim. 6:10).

B. We must trust "in the living God." If we give him first place in our lives, the promise is "all these things shall be added unto you" (Matt. 6:33).

III. The Where of Trust

"He shall cover thee with his feathers, and under his wings shalt thou trust" (Ps. 91:4).

A. Some Christians think they can trust God better while in church or under certain conditions. They often deprive themselves of blessings God wills for them.

B. We can trust God wherever we are—on the mountaintop or in the valley, at home, work, or play. We can dwell, abide, and trust in God (Ps. 91:1–2).

IV. The When of Trust

"Trust ye in the Lord for ever: for in the Lord Jehovah is everlasting strength" (Isa. 26:4).

A. Many trust in God when everything is going good, but when bad times come, they throw up their hands in despair.

B. God wants us to trust him at all times—when troubles, trials, and testings strike as well as in times of tranquility and triumph (Ps. 62:8).

V. The Why of Trust

"The Lord shall help them, and deliver them . . . because they trust in him" (Ps. 37:40).

A. Trust comes before the blessing. We receive God's help because we trust him. Trust comes first.

B. Perfect peace comes through trusting (Isa. 26:3).

21

The Expanse of Praise

Scripture reading: Psalm 148

Text: *"Let them praise the name of the Lord: for his name alone is excellent; his glory is above the earth and heaven"* (Ps. 148:13).

I. The Upward Reach of Praise

"Praise ye the Lord from the heavens: praise him in the heights" (Ps. 148:1).

A. Praise to God reaches beyond the highest peaks. It extends to the heavens and touches the heart of God.

B. The psalmist wrote, "Praise ye him, all his angels: praise ye him, all his hosts" (Ps. 148:2).

C. Many fail to praise the Lord as they should. Since the angels in heaven praise him, we should praise him even more. Heaven is a place of praise to God.

II. The Downward Reach of Praise

"Praise the Lord from the earth" (Ps. 148:7).

A. Our praise to God reaches downward to the discouraged, despondent, and depressed. It lightens the load and lifts the spirit of those who are feeling low.

B. The psalmist said, "Why art thou cast down, O my soul? . . . for I shall yet praise him for the help of his countenance" (Ps. 42:5).

C. Praise to God attracts the lowest of the low. Those who repent and forsake their sins may join in praise to the Lord.

III. The Inward Reach of Praise

"Bless the Lord, O my soul: and all that is within me, bless his holy name" (Ps. 103:1).

A. Praise to God reaches into the heart and soul of God's people. It gives them strength to cope with their innermost needs.

B. Praising the Lord creates a positive attitude and optimistic outlook. It increases faith, hope, and love.

C. The psalmist said, "I delight to do thy will, O my God: yea, thy law is within my heart" (Ps. 40:8). Praise reaches inward.

IV. The Outward Reach of Praise

"Make a joyful noise unto the Lord, all the earth . . . rejoice, and sing praise" (Ps. 98:4).

A. Praise to God should reach around the world. Christians everywhere should praise the Lord for his great love.

B. The psalmist said, "As far as the east is from the west, so far hath he removed our transgressions from us" (Ps. 103:12).

C. Praise enables others to see the joy of the Lord in us, and that should cause them to desire him also.

22

The Love of Money

Scripture reading: 1 Timothy 6:6–12

Text: "For the love of money is the root of all evil" (1 Tim. 6:10).

I. The Desire for Money

"which . . . some coveted after" (1 Tim. 6:10).

A. Most of us desire money, at least to some extent. Money is needed to pay for the necessities of life.

B. We must guard against an excessive love of money and keep a proper perspective concerning it.

C. When the desire for money becomes an all-consuming drive, it is sinful.

D. God's Word admonishes us to "flee these things; and follow after righteousness, godliness, faith, love, patience, meekness" (1 Tim. 6:11).

II. The Deception of Money

"They have erred from the faith" (1 Tim. 6:10).

A. Satan tries to deceive God's people everywhere. His prize tool is the love of money.

B. Satan tempts Christians to love their money and possessions more than they love God.

C. Prayer, perseverance, and the promises of God's Word enable Christians to resist the devil, love God completely, and give him first place in their affections.

D. The scripture urges, "Fight the good fight of faith, lay hold on eternal life" (1 Tim. 6:12).

III. The Destruction Through Money

"and pierced themselves through with many sorrows"
(1 Tim. 6:10).

A. Millions of people have been destroyed by the love of money. They lie, steal, cheat, and even kill for money.

B. Money can be a blessing. It can bring glory to God if used correctly and unselfishly. However, the wrong use of money can bring destruction of body, mind, and soul.

C. The Bible says, "But they that will be rich fall into temptation and a snare, and into many foolish and hurtful lusts, which drown men in destruction and perdition" (1 Tim. 6:9).

D. Let us follow the scriptural admonition to "seek ye first the kingdom of God, and his righteousness; and all these things shall be added unto you" (Matt. 6:33).

23

The Need for Discipline

"But I keep under my body, and bring it into subjection: lest that by any means, when I have preached to others, I myself should be a castaway" (1 Cor. 9:27).

I. Discipline Your Will

"but as the servants of Christ, doing the will of God from the heart" (Eph. 6:6).

A. Discipline means "training that develops self-control . . . acceptance of or submission to authority and control"—Webster.

B. In his most excruciating hour, Jesus submitted his will to his Father's will (Matt. 26:42). We must surrender our will to God's will also. God's will is always best.

II. Discipline Your Ways

"Shew me thy ways, O Lord; teach me thy paths" (Ps. 25:4).

A. Many Christians are set in their ways. They insist on having their own way and fail to be a blessing to others and glorify God.

B. We must submit to God's ways. They produce love, joy, and peace. We are enabled to witness to the lost effectively and to glorify God when our ways please him (Prov. 16:7).

III. Discipline Your Words

"If any man offend not in word, the same is a perfect man, and able also to bridle the whole body" (James 3:2).

A. Some Christians are careless with their tongues. They hurt and discourage new and sensitive Christians with critical and damaging words (Ps. 141:3).

B. We must discipline our words. Be kind, understanding, and strive to increase the confidence of others. Bring healing instead of causing hurt (Eph. 4:32).

IV. Discipline Your Work

"Remembering without ceasing your work of faith, and labour of love. . ." (1 Thess. 1:3).

A. Many Christians neglect to work for God. They are too busy making money and pursuing selfish goals.

B. We must discipline our work, making time to work also for God's cause and kingdom, and helping others.

V. Discipline Your Walk

"As ye have . . . received Christ . . . so walk ye in him" (Col. 2:6).

A. God's Word refers to the Christian life as a "walk." We must discipline our walk so that our influence will cause others to want to live for Christ also.

B. We are to "walk worthy of the Lord unto all pleasing, being fruitful in every good work" (Col. 1:10).

24

You Can M-O-V-E Mountains

"I tell you the truth, if you have faith as small as a mustard seed, you can say to this mountain, 'Move from here to there' and it will move. Nothing will be impossible to you" (Matt. 17:20, NIV).

I. M-otivation Is Needed

"What things soever ye desire, when ye pray, believe that ye receive them, and ye shall have them" (Mark 11:24).

A. Many Christians lack motivation. Merely existing from day to day, they fail to live victoriously.

B. Mountain-moving Christians are motivated by God's love. They possess an inner drive, set goals, and strive to reach them.

C. When Christ's love is lifted up by faith, mountains of doubts and fears come tumbling down (see text).

II. O-bedience Is Needed

"He humbled himself, and became obedient unto death, even the death of the cross" (Phil. 2:8).

A. Christ was obedient unto "even the death of the cross." We must be obedient to God's will for us also.

B. Christ brought victory to the lost through his obedience. He died for our sins, thus removing the mountain of hopelessness for all humankind.

C. Obedience, plus faith, brings victory. When we do God's will with believing faith, mountains of trial, trouble, and testing disappear (Mark 9:23).

III. V-ision Is Needed

"Where there is no vision, the people perish" (Prov. 29:18).

A. Webster says "visualize" means "to form a mental image of something not present to sight."

B. Hebrews 11:1 says it this way: "Faith is the substance of things hoped for, the evidence of things not seen."

C. Through faith Christians can visualize the coming victory. They can win over sin, self, and Satan (1 Cor. 15:57).

IV. E-ndurance Is Needed

"After he had patiently endured, he obtained the promise" (Heb. 6:15).

A. Some Christians are unwilling to wait God's time. They want mountains to move at their own designated time and place.

B. We must endure as Abraham did until "he received the promise." God's timing is always best, never too early or too late.

C. Keep on praying, believing, and waiting for God's timing. Jesus said that believing faith could do the impossible. You can move mountains (Matt. 21:21).

25

Virtues of Faith

"Now faith is the substance of things hoped for, the evidence of things not seen" (Heb. 11:1).

I. The Value of Faith

"But without faith it is impossible to please him" (Heb. 11:6).

A. Some Christians don't realize the value of faith. They can have it, so they think, or do without.

B. The value of faith goes beyond estimation. With faith we can accomplish everything that God wants of us. Without faith we can do little or nothing (Matt. 9:22).

C. Faith is necessary to please God. Faith brings to believers salvation, stability, serenity, and security. Faith is the Christian's lifeline.

II. The Vision of Faith

"Looking unto Jesus the author and finisher of our faith" (Heb. 12:2).

A. Webster says "vision" means "the ability to perceive something not actually visible." Faith is "the evidence of things not seen" (Heb. 11:1).

B. Many Christians lack the vision of faith. They see only the temporal life and its allurements.

C. We must seek to glorify God and be the blessing he

wants us to be. We must look for the good in others, and keep our eyes on Jesus.

III. The Venture of Faith

"Even so faith, if it hath not works, is dead, being alone" (James 2:17).

A. Too many Christians fail to get involved in the venture of faith. They are lax about doing God's work.

B. Christ dared to get involved. He gave his life on the cross for our sins. He took our place, bringing salvation to humankind.

C. Take the venture of faith. Reach out to others with a smile, kind word, good deed, or testimony. James said, "I will shew thee my faith by my works" (James 2:18).

IV. The Victory of Faith

"And this is the victory that overcometh the world, even our faith" (1 John 5:4).

A. Some Christians try to hold on to the world with one hand and to the Lord with the other. They fail.

B. We overcome the world by believing in Jesus Christ (1 John 5:5). The more faith we have, the greater victory we possess.

C. When we know the value of faith, see the vision of faith, take the venture, we experience the victory of faith.

26

What to Expect from God

"My soul, wait thou only upon God; for my expectation is from him. He only is my rock and my salvation: he is my defence; I shall not be moved" (Ps. 62:5–6).

I. Expect Salvation

"He only is my rock and my salvation" (Ps. 62:6).

A. Many people lack a salvation that saves to the uttermost. They profess to be Christians but continue in their old ways.

B. With the psalmist, we should expect a salvation that forgives and cleanses us from our sins and keeps us pure and holy.

C. The apostle Paul said, "Therefore if any man be in Christ, he is a new creature: old things are passed away; behold, all things are become new" (2 Cor. 5:17).

D. When a Christian makes a total surrender to God, the Holy Spirit purifies his heart, directs his life, and keeps that which he has committed to him (2 Tim. 1:12).

II. Expect Safekeeping

"He is my defence" (Ps. 62:6).

A. The psalmist was definite about God's protective care. He said of the Lord, "He is my refuge and my fortress: my God; in him will I trust" (Ps. 91:2).

B. We must expect God's safekeeping also. In today's world, where there is trouble, turmoil, and terrorism, we need God's protective care at all times.

C. God often directly intervenes for his children. Sometimes he sends his angels to watch over and guard his trusting ones.

D. The psalmist said, "For he shall give his angels charge over thee, to keep thee in all thy ways" (Ps. 91:11).

III. Expect Stability

"I shall not be moved" (Ps. 62:6).

A. Some Christians are wishy-washy, up one day and down the next. You never know where to find them. They are unhappy and unfruitful.

B. God wants us to become established and productive. He offers stability through prayer, his Word, self-discipline, and faith.

C. Peter said, "But the God of all grace . . . after that ye have suffered a while, make you perfect, stablish, strengthen, settle you" (1 Peter 5:10).

D. Trust God. Expect salvation, safekeeping, and stability. "For my expectation is from him" (Ps. 62:5).

27

Why God's Word Is Great

"For the word of God is quick, and powerful, and sharper than any two-edged sword" (Heb. 4:12).

I. Great Because of Its Source

"All scripture is given by inspiration of God" (2 Tim. 3:16).

A. The Bible is God's written word to us. God spoke to the faithful who diligently recorded his Word.

B. Some have denied the truth of God's Word, but it has continued to stand the test of time. It is still the best-selling book.

C. False prophets have ridiculed the principles for which the Word of God stands. God's truth still shines through the darkness like a never-failing beacon (Ps. 119:105).

D. God is the source of his Word. The Bible tells humankind of his love, hope, and assurance of eternal life through Jesus Christ.

II. Great Because of Its Course

"Go ye into all the world, and preach the gospel to every creature" (Mark 16:15).

A. Man sinned and deserved to die. "For the wages of sin is death; but the gift of God is eternal life through Jesus Christ our Lord" (Rom. 6:23).

B. To be saved we must come to God just as we are in

simple, trusting faith. We must repent of our sins and believe in Christ for salvation.

C. The course of God's Word is "into all the world." "God so loved the world, that he gave his only begotten Son, that whosoever believeth in him should not perish, but have everlasting life" (John 3:16).

D. No one need be left out. All are included in salvation's plan—the black and white, young and old, rich and poor, great and small.

III. Great Because of Its Force

"piercing even to the dividing asunder of soul and spirit" (Heb. 4:12).

A. Steam power, horse power, water power, even atomic power cannot compare with the power of God's Word. It surpasses them all.

B. God's Word is great because of its force. Earthly power may kill and destroy, but it cannot bring peace of mind and spirit. God spoke the universe, humankind, and all creation into existence.

C. God's Word says, "He is able also to save them to the uttermost that come unto God by him" (Heb. 7:25).

D. The power of God's Word reaches the lowest of the low and sets them free from the clutches of sin.

28

Win with Patience

"In your patience possess ye your souls" (Luke 21:19).

I. Wait with Patience

"I waited patiently for the Lord; and he inclined unto me, and heard my cry" (Ps. 40:1).

A. Waiting is difficult for most and worse for some. Many Christians lack patience in this area of their lives. They want what they want when they want it.

B. If we are to please God and live victorious lives, we must learn to patiently wait for God's timing. It takes time for him to answer some of our prayers, but he knows best when to grant the answers.

C. The psalmist admonished, "Rest in the Lord, and wait patiently for him: fret not thyself" (Ps. 37:7).

II. Work with Patience

"For ye have need of patience, that, after ye have done the will of God, ye might receive the promise" (Heb. 10:36).

A. Patience is required when it comes to doing God's work. The results may be slow in coming.

B. We should work for God patiently and willingly, giving him first place in our lives, seeking to do those things which please him.

C. Col. 3:17 teaches: "And whatsoever ye do in word

or deed, do all in the name of the Lord Jesus, giving thanks to God."

III. Walk with Patience

"For we walk by faith, not by sight" (2 Cor. 5:7).

A. The Bible often refers to our life as a walk. We should therefore walk (live) by faith, not by sight.
B. According to Col. 2:6: "As ye have therefore received Christ Jesus the Lord, so walk ye in him."
C. A patient walk results in victory. "Rooted and built up in him, and established in the faith . . . abounding therein with thanksgiving" (Col. 2:7).

IV. Watch with Patience

"The Lord direct your hearts into the love of God, and into the patient waiting for Christ" (2 Thess. 3:5).

A. We must watch with patience for Christ's return. When man's predictions fail, people often are tempted to lose faith in the second coming.
B. Nevertheless, we must continue to watch for his coming with diligence. "Watch therefore; for ye know not what hour your Lord doth come" (Matt. 24:42, 44).
C. Jesus promised it so we know it is true. He said, "I will come again, and receive you unto myself; that where I am, there ye may be also" (John 14:3). Watch with patience.